MW01122095

Power of Color

# Growing Green

# A Garden of Natural Paint Colors

## Sally Fretwell's New Paint Colors

www.sallyfretwell.com

For more information please contact Sally Fretwell
toll free at 888-830-1860
email to sally@sallyfretwell.com
sydfarrar@sallyfretwell.com
or visit www.sallyfretwell.com

Library of Congress Cataloguing-In-Publication Data
        Sally Fretwell

        Interior Design, Interior Decorating, Architectural Consulting, Home
        Building, Home Remodeling, Use of Colors

                1. Interior Design  2. Interior Decorating  3. Architectural
                Consulting  4. Home Remodeling  5. Architectural Psychology
                6. Feng Shui

        ISBN 0-9721548-9-2

        Sally Fretwell. -- 1st Edition




Printed in Canada

Editor: Syd Farrar
Graphics and Photo Editing: John C G Thompson
Cover Design: Sally Fretwell and John C G Thompson
Page Design and Layout: John C G Thompson

## Acknowledgements:

Thanks to Bruce for sharing with me his love of color, his paint formulation skills and his vast knowledge of the paint business.

Thanks to Syd for being my partner in business and helping me keep focused on selling great paint products and having happy customers.

Thanks to John for his photography skills with his photographer's eye for the perfect shot and for all his help in creating my vision of a book full of color for people to enjoy.

Thanks to our customers, past and future, whose warm embrace of my colors and paint have made all the work worthwhile.

# WHY A FLOWER COLOR BOOK?

Flowers naturally invoke a response for many reasons. Each of the multitude of species of flowers, although different, all seem as they were perfectly put together. There are no bad flowers nor are there bad flower colors. Each flower, with its individual form, structure and color, speaks to us in different ways.

One of my favorites is the simple crocus that stubbornly decides to show itself in late winter or early spring. It is as if to say, "Here I am, it is time to rumble, time to show myself", and regardless of the weather decides to push its simple, frail stem through the snow to announce itself with a beautiful bloom. The picture of the crocus says it all. It shows the power of a flower to break through the bleakness of winter, to reaffirm that we have survived another winter and spring is on its way. This bleak backdrop for a simple, vividly colored flower reminds us of the cycle of life and can elicit a chuckle, a smile and a sense of wonderment that if the crocus can do it then so can we. Similar responses come when we see beautiful green, lush mosses adapting and surviving on the seaside rocks of the Maine coastline and colorfully flourishing.

In Little Compton, Rhode Island, I would visit my Grandmother during the summer. The beach and seaside of that locale was so different from any other place I ever visited. The sand was of a different texture from normal beachside sand. We walked to the beach through sea grasses and along paths of naturally growing wildflowers with textures and colors that were atypical to a beach area. The smell of flowers mixed with the salty beach air was different. There were ocean-side cliffs, sculpted by thousands of years of pounding waves and on these cliffs were huge patches of green moss that had adapted to the ocean water instead of fresh water.

It was a beautiful place that I can see and remember as clearly today as when I first walked those seaside paths. I still cherish the remembrances of those unique sights, smells, tastes and sounds. Today when I see color like the dark green moss or flowers of Little Compton, all those pleasant memories coming rushing back to me. Flower colors can elicit similar response and memories. That is why colors are so important when deciding on painting a room, house or home. The colors that you love serve as more than just colors but serve as a bouquet of memories. Picking the right color for your wall is not just about getting the right color. It is also about picking colors that elicit a positive response. Like a vase of freshly cut flowers from your garden, the perfectly picked warm room color will add a fresh spot of cheer to your home. That is the reason for this book of warm colors pulled from the natural beauty of flowers. It is my attempt to bring the power of flower colors into your life.

*"Like a vase of fresh cut flowers"*

# The Science of Color

*Why another color book you might ask?*

The answer is simple: to introduce new paint colors and to share with you what I have learned from working with my retail paint store customers, professional painters and consultation clients.

Before I had developed my line of paints, I would do a home consultation, pick colors from a fan deck, (a collection of 1" x 1/2 "color swatches) for a client and be on my way. Now this process is much more involved and intimate so to speak. I am still picking the colors for a room, whole houses, restaurants and commercial buildings. Instead of using fan decks, I use color boards or my answer to the fan deck a paint stick which is the actual color (two coats) on a large 5 gallon paint stirrer. Instead of a printers ink on paper, I can now show a customer the actual paint pigment on a painted surface. Then I mix the paint at my shop. After the painting crew has done their magic, I usually get to see the end result. This start to finish color process from exploration to completion has been an extremely interesting experience. It has allowed me to further educate myself about paint colors and why people choose the colors they do. Being allowed into the mind and soul of a client has been enlightening and I have learned that color and choosing color can bring up a vast array of feelings, memories and emotions.

Listening to the clients express their desires is the first step to bringing them to the place where they can find what they are looking for.  Many times it is hard for them verbalize what it is they want.  They can't express it.  It is sort of like saying, "I know what I want when I find it." But in order to have a starting point, I have had to draw out of them some sort of description of what they are seeking.  Many people are nervous about picking colors.  In the past they have gone to a paint store, picked a color from a fan deck, had the paint store mix the paint, took it home, put it on the wall and then realized that it was not anything like the color they had envisioned.  After this has happened several times they get it in their mind that they can not pick color.  Nothing is further from the truth.

We can, with the right guidance, pick colors that are right for us and our surroundings.  Most people do not realize that in the normal paint color picking process many outside influences conspire against picking the right color.  The normal fan deck has a row of similar colors or shades.  When you look at  a fan deck, your mind's eye sees not only the color you are considering but also the surrounding colors.  Result: You are not visually seeing a true representation of the color you are focusing on. With this working against you, it is no wonder that when you take a paint color home and put it on your wall, it does not always look like the color you had picked.

We have made picking a color more chooser friendly.  It is like the proverbial light bulb going on.  All of a sudden clients begin to not only "see" colors but "feel" them also. On a consultation, at a client's home or in my store, the process of hearing their thoughts, fears, wants, and desires gets the ball rolling.

Our goal is to create an easier method to feel confident about picking paint colors. We want to give customers the ability to experiment with colors that work for them. The first color chosen

is not always the color that ends up on the wall. Whether at home or in the store we want customers to be able to see the paint on our paint sticks. We encourage them to take the stick home, lay it on the wall, look at that color under the different lighting of morning, noon and night in order to get a feel for the color. We want them to get a response from the color that can only comes from seeing that color on a wall as they move throughout their house. We have found that this creates an ease with choosing the proper color of paint. What was once stressful becomes much less worrisome and more relaxed. The individual gains an understanding of what they are looking for and what will bring life into a space.

From my architectural psychologist standpoint, the truly fun part of my business is seeing the customer's emotional response to a color. They are happier with the right colors. Just as people will cringe when they see a color that is clearly too stark or a color that is not for them, the opposite is true when they find a perfect match not only for their wall but their soul. I hear comments like, "I never thought I could feel this good in my home"; "You have to experience this for yourself, please come over"; "I can't believe that all my photos look so good now"; "The paint color made my floors pop"; and my favorite, "The yellow we chose for the kitchen scared me at first but now I sit there and soak up the light every morning!"

All of these statements came from clients who initially expressed doubt that color could really make a difference. Many clients only chose subtle shades of colors that they already felt comfortable with. When they were introduced to a larger group of colors, their response was positive. It was easy to explain to them that many times soft or pastel colors are not filled with enough pigment, thus they lack enough of the primary colors that impart color to all tones. They are weak and dull colors. Thus they have little or no drawing power. When the color is right, it will have enough pigment to draw in natural sunlight, warming up a space.

"I never thought I could feel this good in my home"

Picking paint colors can be easy

New 2008 Colors to follow

Adobe

Going Green

Poinsetta

Out on a Limb

# Warm and Inviting Spaces

Everyone knows of places they have been or visited where they felt uplifted. It might have been a restaurant, a favorite store, an exotic vacation destination, a friend's home or your childhood home. My goal as an architectural psychologist is to work with clients to create such places in their own home and work space.

Much of my foundation of this work is based on my studies with psychology. I look at the practical and easily understandable examples of how color, lighting and space can influence your life. My third book, entitled *The Power of Color*, was my first attempt at actually picking colors that visually expressed a feeling and a sense of warmth and comfort. Those who read the book and saw the colors asked if there was any way that they could get the colors in the book made into paint colors. That started the ball rolling. I now have my own unique line of environmentally friendly, No-VOC paints. It has been a wonderful journey and experience for me. I now have almost 140 colors, including 40 new colors featured in this book.

I do not think that anyone needs a color forecaster from New York to tell them what colors will be "hot" for 2008 or 2009. Forecaster[1]s attempt to predict trends and we all know trends come and go. My colors are right outside my door. The warm, rejuvenating and inspiring colors of nature are my palette. If you love the natural beauty of the first spring crocus pushing itself through a groundcover of snow then you will understand where I am coming from. I did not make these colors, they have been around forever, created by a power much greater than my own. I have humbly pulled these colors, in all their natural beauty and warmth, and have attempted to put them into a paint form, that you can use in your own home or work place.

Glow Bug

French Bloom

# Neutral Colors

People often want to choose light, neutral or pastel tones to paint rooms in their home. Choosing these tones often brings about mixed results. A quick glance at a typical fan deck will show you that light or pastel colors often lack enough color pigmentation to bring life to a room. This does not mean you have to use darker colors. It does mean that you should be careful when choosing lighter colors to insure that they have "pulling power" or enough pigment to draw in natural sunlight and warm up a room.

Off-whites, tans and neutral colors often feel dead and lifeless on a wall. Featured in the previous three pictures is a typical Virginia home, built in the 1950's with a traditional Williamsburg white, wall coloring with a gray or dark trim. In the second picture the same hall has been painted. It is evident that the neutral color, *"Faded Stucco"*, adds a warm glow to this hall landing and is perfectly complemented by a creamy, white trim that is not too tan or too blue. The trim and wall color brighten the room. The flooring and railings were untouched but because the paint color draws in and holds light, it creates a positive influence on everything that surrounds it. The hallway pictured has a warm glow on dark, dreary days or nights because of its pigment, tone and warmth.

Breezy Green

Sea Oat

Sea Foam

Low Tide

Sea Glass

# TRIM COLOR

Most people know what they like when they see it. They may not know why they like it or be able to define what it is they like but they just know they like it. I have many customers who love color and know they want uplifting colors for their walls. It has been my experience in working with these customers that they often overlook a very important factor in getting just the right colors for their home. Trim color is crucial. People underestimate the importance of trim in the overall feeling of a room. It is the accent to the perfect wall color and completes the space.

Builders construct spec homes with the intention of being neutral and often do not realize that their trim paint is usually a cold, stark white paint with white-blue tones that are mentally depressing and thus give the appearance of being cheap and shoddy. Older homes can also suffer from the same situation where the paint is colder in tone. These spaces need a warmer paint color to bring them alive.

White is normally the color homeowner's use for trim. Stark, white trim with blue overtones can have the same effect as dark colored trim. Most homeowners know instinctively that something is not right but can not always put a finger on it. They might like a room color but for them the room is not "popping" like it should, because they are relying on an old unsuccessful custom of decorating.

When I show a client a warm white in a side-by-side comparison to their cold white, they immediately see the difference. They can see that the warmer tones add life. It fades into the wall color

and becomes complementary with the dominant color and not a stark contrast to it. Warm white trim helps give the room an expansive feel. It can open up a vista by leading the eye out beyond the room.

The goal with the trim is to softly define the room and to support the wall colors. I have found from experience that finding a warm white that is not too tan or yellow is not always easy. However, it is important for the wall colors in your home that you find one. Picking and painting the trim color is always extra work. It seems an unimportant afterthought but, in the end, it can make or break the project.

Castle Green

Tuscan Tan

Rock Garden

Autumn Field

Wheat Grass

Grey Sands

Blue Lagoon

Santa Fe

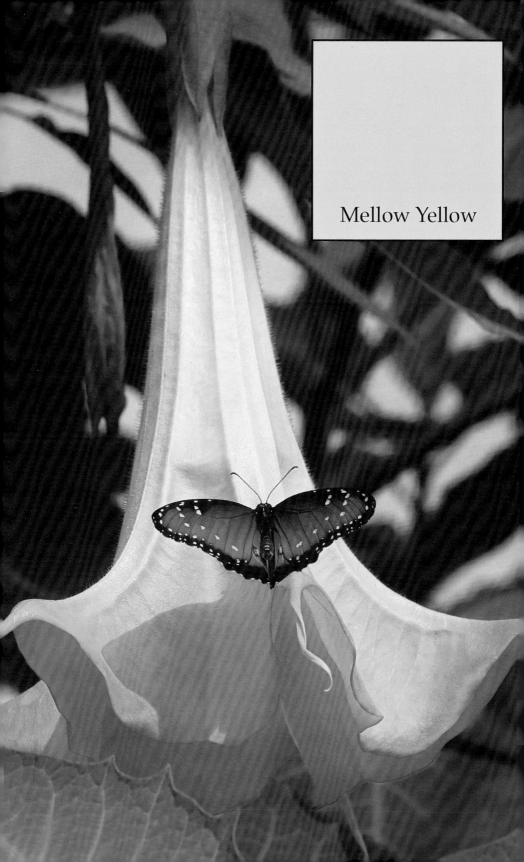

Mellow Yellow

# Nature's Combinations

Nature offers us a plethora of combinations of colors that one may not consider when decorating. This is why I love to pull my colors from pictures of nature and natural settings. The lilac breasted roller, in the photograph, proudly displays a stunning blue and lavender combination of feathers. Would anyone ever consider painting a wall this light blue and complement it with lavender pillows or a bed quilt? The reason these two colors look so good together is because they are both warm tones which allow for a working combination.

Whether or not you like these colors is a personal preference. They are full-bodied, with strong color pigmentation depth and warmth. The colors have a "wow" factor and play well together. Colors will change when put next to other colors, thus the same colors in different settings can look completely different. If you have ever done any knitting you will observe that the same piece of yarn used to knit one scarf can look completely different when it is used on another scarf and combined with different colors of yarn. Fashion and clothes designers use this concept all the time. You can also, when picking colors for your home or office.

If you like cooler colors you need to balance them with warm colors. Lavenders and blues are tough colors to make warmer. Since blue is cold in itself, adding other colors that have warmth or adding warm tones of blue, allow blue to be a wonderful color in decorating. I often use the example of ocean blue. Taken by itself, it is a cool or cold color, but taken as a whole with its surroundings – the sun, sand, tropical beach umbrellas, colorful towels, island flowers – the coolness of the ocean is warmed by all that surrounds it.

Many clients have rugs they want to work with when trying to choose colors for their home. They spend many painstaking and endless hours trying to find paint colors that will work on their walls and complement their rug. Often oriental rugs have cold blues, maroons or dark greens, all cold colors that are not good for drawing out a good wall color. Rugs can dictate how a room will feel and sometimes it is best to pick a wall color first and then find a rug that will highlight that color. If the rug has already been bought, then we must work to see what colors and tones can be pulled out to enhanced and complemented the wall color.

It is the same in kitchens with their granite, tile, stone work or cabinets that are already in place. Granites and stone have a natural beauty that is revealed when the right paint color is picked. It takes work and a keen eye but if done correctly it can add a "pop" to your kitchen and bring out a depth and beauty that was not present until the correct wall color was chosen.

A client asked me to her home because she had redone her bathroom, picking new tile and granite as well as a backsplash. All were very nice materials when considered individually. Each exuded multi-colored facets that you could pull colors from for a wall color. Once they were put into the bathroom, she was so exasperated to find that the three did not look good together. In theory, all should have worked fine together. The problem was the color on the wall had to be picked from a very narrow range of colors to make the components work together. We found only one color looked good with all three. All of the color families worked with one but looked horrible with the others, thus making it look like she had not given real thought to her tile and stone choices. The paint color we chose enhanced the relationship between the tile and granite. In the end everything worked well together. If she had picked the paint color first, this would not have happened.

"Often oriental rugs have cold blues, maroons or dark greens, all cold colors that are not good for drawing out a good wall color."

Spring Red

Daisy

Paradise Green

Hybiscus

# COLORS THAT ALWAYS WORK FOR YOU!

All colors, be it a blue, green, red, yellow or even fuchsia have cool and warm tones. Paint colors that are predominantly warm are softer on the eyes and blend well with other colors. They make a color statement but don't overpower the room. They are always useable as a wall color. Strong colors with cool tones are overpowering, because they are harsher than warmer tones. After painting a cool tone, your immediate reaction is to want to "tone it down". It is not the boldness or strength of a color that makes people cringe when looking at such tones. Stark, bold colors with predominantly cool tones reflect natural light preventing these cool colors from having a relationship with the colors around them. Bright reds, strong oranges, intense blues can be used as wall colors if you employ the warmer tones of these colors. When they exhibit warmer tones, they become a part of the mood, becoming a room that people love to be in.

Ginger Tea

Fruit Punch

# The Color White

There are so many shades of "white". There are off whites, Navaho whites, snow whites, antique whites and milk whites, just to name a few. The name of the white does not matter because it is the tone of the white that makes all the difference. Some white tones are too brown, too grey, or too blue.

Finding a warm white for use as a trim or ceiling coler is not always easy. Most builders use a contractor's white. It is a stark, cold and dreary white. It often clashes, with grey white trim and blue white ceilings. When I point out these differences in white to a client, they can easily see the clash. These white "colors" were not carefully chosen.

To show a client the difference the color of white can make, I once painted a small piece of trim under a granite countertop. It was a stark white that fought with the granite, drawing attention to the trim instead of the beautiful countertop. On another section of trim, I painted a warm white trim. The difference was immediately evident. The warm white trim caused the trim piece to disappear and drew the eye to the beautiful countertop, thus creating a more upscale look. This is a simple way to add value to your home.

*"This is a simple way to add value to your home."*

Butterscotch

Coffee Bean

# No VOC Paint
# Non toxic Paint

The paint industry is formulating less toxic paints. The public has demanded it and the paint companies are listening. *No VOC* is the buzz word. What does *No VOC* mean? VOC is an acronym for volatile organic compound. Paint is made up of organic and inorganic compounds. For the most part, organic compounds are released when paint is taken out of the can and applied to a wall. Some of the organic compounds are solvents or other toxic materials. They are usually associated with "paint smell".

Many of these toxins are both harsh on the body and the environment. These toxins are a cause of ozone depletion which is associated with global warming. If you are around paint that is NOT of a "no-" or "low-VOC" type, you can absorb the airborne toxins into your body. Many people with weak immune systems, lung or liver problems, can have a hard time removing these toxins from their body. They can cause headaches, allergic reactions, aches and pains. They are especially hard on individuals who suffer from asthma and other respiratory problems.

Excellent research and product development by paint manufacturing companies has allowed them to find non-toxic substitutes for toxic materials normally used in paint. No longer does using a "No VOC" paint means you have to sacrifice good coverage, full-bodied colors or long lasting paint. With the elimination of volatile organic compounds, you no longer have to be worried about the headaches and breathing problems that are often associated with being in a newly painted room. "No VOC" does not mean "no odor" but it does mean that there no harmful emissions.

Many specialty paints and primers still have toxins and strong chemicals. It is always a good idea to ask for help when you purchase paint so that you fully understand the ingredients in the paint that you purchase. Paints containing toxins are not bad paints they just contain ingredients that are bad for you.

Hydrangea

Spring Green

Aussi Orange

Lazy Day

Poppy Passion

# Granite, Tile , Cork and Natural Stone

It has been a common theme in many design and home style magazines to highlight the "go green" movement. These articles often discuss the use of various granite, stones and tiles that have natural pigments and tones. These surfaces exude their own natural warmth and are a lot of fun to pull wall colors from.

Many times a person falls in love with a specific granite or marble for use in a kitchen or bathroom. They come to me to see what colors they can use to complement their stone choice. We start pulling paint sticks of my colors looking for a match. It is always a pleasant surprise, like finding a coin on the street, to find something that was unexpected. When we find the right color, the reaction is invariably, "Wow, look at that!" Until they are shown the colors that oftentimes exist, they are not able to imgine the vast array of colors before their very eyes.

Wall paint colors can be easily chosen to accentuate the natural beauty in flooring products. One client specifically loved cork flooring. She found a very upscale pattern which was filled with colors that caught the eye. She owned a retail store and wanted to use the cork flooring to impress customers as soon as they walked in the door. Her goal was to pick a wall color that would make the floor "pop".

We found that certain colors really made the lighter colors in the cork pop out, while other paint colors brought out darker tones and shades. She took my paint sticks to her new store location where the floor had been installed and discovered that her options were limitless. She now had positive options about the feeling that she wanted to convey to her customers. The choice was hers.

Often clients who buy homes with existing cabinets, counter tops and flooring in their new homes have a problem with the standard contractor's white paint. They want to know how they can make the best of an uncomfortable situation. I work with them to find colors that accentuate the beauty in the cabinets and build a bridge between the counter top, cabinets and flooring.

New homeowners love certain aspects of their home but long for color and warmth. Finding a wall color that brings the counter tops, cabinets and the natural beauty in the floor alive, is the key. A big factor is the trim color that already exists in a home whether it an old or new. Trim color totally changes how a room will feel. Simply changing a blue-ish white colored trim that exists in many old and new homes to a warm, creamy white trim will create a new found ambiance that will help pull a room together.

The moral of this story is that, in many cases, small adjustments and awareness to what you have can make all the difference. Sometimes a huge over haul is not needed. A keen eye, to see what needs to be emphasized and complemented, is sometimes all that is needed to provide an inexpensive but wonderful fix to a bad match of flooring, counter tops and cabinets. A few gallons of paint can make all the difference in the overall feel of a room.

When we find the right color, the reaction is invariably, "Wow, look at that!"

# Moo-ve into Color!

Cowtail

# Painters and Prep Work

Your paint job is only as good as your painter. If you are like me and end up wearing more paint than you put on the wall, it might be good to seek professional help. If you are a good painter, I envy you and you can skip this brief installment of hopefully helpful painting tips.

Ultimately, how good your paint color looks on the wall, to a large extent, depends on prepping and priming before painting. New dry wall always needs to be primed. There are no exceptions. The primer seals and supports the finished color and acts as a platform for any color you may choose. Old and dirty walls need to be primed to insure a uniformity of color. Walls with nicks, holes or other irregularities need to be replastered, sanded and primed. Bathroom walls, even if they look clean probably need to be primed due to the presence of hairspray, aerosols and moisture in a bathroom environment. Aerosol use and moisture concentrations often remain hidden until painted. Splotchy paint coloration can appear with the application of new paint. This effect makes the paint appear to literally "crawl" up the walls. Make sure your painters take precautions to prevent this.

To achieve a successful result you will have to apply several coats of paint. Sometimes partially tinting a primer with the same color helps to achieve the depth of color you seek by requiring fewer coats. Tinted primers are also useful if you are painting over a strong or dark color. Stronger colors take more tint. Heavily tinted paint often causes dilution of the titanium dioxide component and thus makes the paint thinner. This also may cause a need for additional coats of paint.

When getting quotes from a professional painter, always make sure you ask how many coats of paint they are quoting when they give you a price. Ask them if this includes a coat of primer. Ask them if they are providing the primer or is the primer being supplied by you. You want all quotes to reflect the same amount of work and paint or primer being used. Be aware that when working with stronger colors you will probably need a minimum of two coats and some require three. Make sure that the added labor and time of extra coats is taken into account in your paint quote. Some painters are not comfortable with strong colors so make sure that you inform the painter of your color choices before the quote is finalized.

You can have the best primer, paint and paint colors, but unless you are a great painter or have a qualified professional painter your paint job could end up looking less than stellar. When using professional painters always ask for references and check them. Most good paint stores will have painters they recommend and stand behind those recommendations.

Siena

Sun Drenched

Copper Sea

# Excitement from Color

I love the satisfaction I feel when watching clients get excited in the color choosing process. I know the color choices will have a positive psychological impact on them when they are living and working in those rooms.

I hope that, in my books, you will find colors that are special to you, inspire you,  bring you memories of wonderful times past or colors that can build memories for the future.  I hope to enable you to look at color in a different light, to understand how a color can positively affect your life and in doing so make you want to bring color into your life. I am sure you will enjoy the experience as much as I have.

*Using the right colors, along with complimentary lighting and your own personal touch, any space can become an enjoyable and rejuvenating space to be in."*

It is our feeling that paint has become a commodity and is being sold not for its color properties but for its price. Our model emphasizes color, making the choice easy.

We are working to build a different kind of paint store model that is as much about color as it is about paint. We want our store to make the color picking process easy and enjoyable. We have introduced our paint line to owners of furniture stores, interior decorating shops and flooring stores. They know what it is like to work with clients in trying to create wonderful spaces to live and work in. They love the idea of selling paint themselves thus adding to their goal of being a full service interior design provider.

Coastal Green

Go Green

Going Green

Gone Green

Sally Fretwell Paint Colors
Sold at
Power of Color in Richmond, VA
Paint Plus in Charlottesville, VA
Davis Frost in Lynchburg, VA
Nunnally's Flooring in Wawsaw, VA
Tal-y-bont in Morehead City, NC
Old Town Supply in Cheraw, SC
My Green Cottage in Reston, VA
for other locations please visit

www.sallyfretwell.com

# The Sally Fretwell Paint Colors Team

John Thompson, photographer and graphic specialist 434-971-8253

Bruce Butler, Color formulations and paint expert, owner of Paint Plus Charlottesville, VA 434-973-8344

Sally Fretwell, architectural psychologist, author, owner

Syd Farrar, writer, editor, owner
sydfarrar@sallyfretwell.com

# Photo copyrights

Wren Farrar:107
John Thompson: Cover, 20, 22, 24,110,111
www.iStockphoto.com/achiartistul:11
"/aimintang:76
"/Anettelinnea:28
"/Aprioril:94
"/Blackjake:52
"/Brazzo:70
"/cacafuegos:42
"/crazyD:12
"/creativeaimage:35
"/danbreckwoldt:100
"/Dewitt:96
"/Emble:1
"/Elpiniki:3
"/EricVega:17
"/Evgenyb:6
"/eyecrave: Cover, 58
"/farbenrausch:93
"/fotow:80
"/hkuchera:45
"/JFTringali:44
"/JGould:30
"/jordanchez:75
"/jumpphotography:87
"/JuniperCreek:14
"/jurgaR:50, 60
"/Kcastagnola:68

# Photo copyrights *continued*

"/Lauriek:5
"/lijlexmom:85,88"
"/marmoin:90
"/maica:99
"/mcveras:54
"/mschowe:56
"/naphtalina:38
"/nnehring:66
"/00Y00:Cover
"/peskymonkey:26
"/peteraustin:79
"/photogal:62
"/pinobarile:32
"/pinksel:37
"/pinobarile:104
"/pjmalsloury:46
"/poiremolle:73
"/scoobydoo2:82
"/Sundikov:8
"/sviridov-0:49
"/syagci:78
"/tirc:83
"/TNOTN:40
"/trigger photo:102
"/Valskovaya:109
"/Vera-g:18

Sally Fretwell is certified by the American Society of Interior Designers to teach her continuing education classes.   She is also available for consultation.

Sally Fretwell

1-888-830-1860

sally@sallyfretwell.com

Power of Color store
Richmond VA
804-726-5091